SEO FOR E-COMMERCE

Strategies for Increasing Visibility to Build Long-Term Traffic & Sales

Danielle Mead

CONTENTS

INTRODUCTION

When I first started working with e-commerce clients, one of the most common questions I heard was, "Why isn't my store getting traffic?" Many store owners assume that simply launching a website and listing their products is enough to start generating sales. But without search engine optimization (SEO), an e-commerce site is like a store tucked away in an alley with no signage – no one knows it exists. SEO is the key to driving organic traffic to your online store, helping you reach customers who are actively searching for what you sell.

Why SEO Matters for E-Commerce

The e-commerce landscape is more competitive than ever. With thousands of online stores selling similar products, standing out in search results can make the difference between thriving and struggling. Unlike paid advertising, which stops working the moment you stop paying, SEO creates is a foundation for consistent long-term traffic. A well-optimized store can generate consistent, high-quality traffic without the ongoing cost of ads.

Think about how you shop online. When you need a product, you likely turn to Google, type in what you're looking for, and click on one of the first few results. Your potential customers do the same. If your store isn't ranking on the first page for relevant keywords, you're missing out on sales. SEO ensures that when people search for the products you sell, your store appears where it matters most.

Beyond just rankings, SEO also improves user experience. A well-structured site with clear navigation, fast load times, and relevant content helps customers find what they need quickly. Google rewards these elements with higher rankings, meaning a well-optimized site not only attracts visitors but also converts them into buyers.

The Challenges of E-Commerce SEO vs. Standard Website SEO

E-commerce SEO comes with unique challenges that set it apart from optimizing a standard website or blog. The first major hurdle is product page optimization. Unlike a blog, where content is long-form and keyword-rich, product pages often have minimal text, making it harder to rank. Store owners must find ways to incorporate valuable keywords naturally without making descriptions feel forced or "written for SEO".

Another common challenge is duplicate content. Many e-commerce sites fall into the trap of copying manufacturer descriptions or using similar content across multiple product pages. Search engines penalize duplicate content, making it essential to write unique, engaging product descriptions for each item.

Site structure and crawlability also present issues. E-commerce stores typically have hundreds, if not thousands, of product pages, categories, and filters. Without proper site architecture, search engines may struggle to crawl and index your pages efficiently. Optimizing internal linking, using canonical tags, and ensuring a logical URL structure are crucial to making your store search-engine friendly.

Then there's the issue of competition. If you're selling products in a highly competitive niche, ranking for broad, high-volume keywords can be incredibly difficult. Instead, e-commerce SEO requires a strategic approach – targeting long-tail keywords, leveraging content marketing, and earning high-quality backlinks to gain authority over time.

Who This Book Is For

This book is written for anyone who wants to grow their e-commerce business through SEO. Whether you're a store owner managing your own website, a marketer looking to improve organic traffic, or a web developer responsible for site structure and technical SEO, the strategies in this book will help you improve visibility and drive sales.

If you're an e-commerce entrepreneur, this book

will teach you how to optimize your product pages, improve rankings, and attract customers who are ready to buy.

If you're a digital marketer, you'll learn advanced strategies to outperform competitors, from content marketing to structured data and backlink building.

If you're a developer, you'll discover best practices for optimizing site architecture, improving page speed, and ensuring search engines can effectively crawl your site.

Regardless of your role, this book is designed to be practical, providing actionable steps rather than vague theory. My goal is to break down SEO into digestible, easy-to-follow strategies so you can start seeing results.

How to Use This Book

SEO can feel overwhelming, especially for e-commerce store owners juggling multiple responsibilities. That's why this book is structured in a way that allows you to work through it at your own pace.

In the first section, we'll cover the fundamentals of SEO, ensuring you have a solid understanding of how search engines work and what factors impact rankings. From there, we'll dive into on-page optimization, covering everything from product pages to site structure. We'll also explore technical SEO, content marketing strategies, link building, and advanced tactics that can give you a competitive edge.

Each chapter includes practical examples, real-world case studies, and step-by-step instructions. I encourage you to implement what you learn as you go. SEO is not a one-time fix – it's an ongoing process that requires testing, tweaking, and adapting to algorithm changes. By the end of this book, you'll have a complete SEO strategy tailored specifically for your e-commerce business, giving you the tools to grow your organic traffic and increase sales.

Whether you're new to SEO or looking to refine your current strategy, this book will serve as your guide to mastering e-commerce SEO. Let's get started!

PART 1: SEO FUNDAMENTALS FOR E-COMMERCE

UNDERSTANDING SEARCH ENGINES & SEO BASICS

When I first started diving into SEO, it seemed like a complicated game – one where the rules kept changing. But at its core, SEO is about making sure your store is visible to the right people at the right time. To do that, you need to understand how search engines work. Google, Bing, and other search engines have one main goal: to deliver the most relevant and useful results to users. If your online store isn't optimized, search engines won't see it as the best result, and you'll struggle to rank where customers can find you.

How Search Engines Work: Crawling, Indexing, and Ranking

Imagine a massive library filled with billions of books, but instead of a librarian organizing them, a search engine uses automated bots – known as crawlers – to scan and categorize them. When you create a new e-commerce store or add a new product page, these crawlers explore your site, reading its content and structure. This process is called crawling.

Once crawlers analyze your site, they store that information in a massive database, known as the index. This is where Google "remembers" your website and its content so it can retrieve it later when someone searches for relevant terms.

The final step is ranking. When a user searches for a keyword like "best wireless headphones," search engines sift through their index and rank results based on hundreds of factors. These include keyword relevance, site speed, mobile-friendliness, backlinks, and user experience. SEO is the practice of optimizing your site so it ranks as high as possible in search results, ideally on page one.

If your store isn't properly structured for crawling and indexing, your products might never appear in search results. One of the best ways to help search engines understand your site is by submitting an XML sitemap in Google Search Console. This acts like a roadmap, guiding crawlers through your most important pages and ensuring they get indexed correctly.

Key Google Algorithm Updates That Affect E-Commerce SEO

Google is constantly tweaking its algorithms to improve search results. While minor updates happen regularly, certain major changes have significantly impacted e-commerce SEO over the years. Understanding these updates can help you avoid common pitfalls and adjust your strategy accordingly.

Panda Update (2011) – Content Quality Matters

Before this update, many e-commerce sites used "thin" or duplicate content to rank. Panda penalized sites that had copied product descriptions, keyword stuffing, or low-quality content. If you're using generic manufacturer descriptions, this could hurt your rankings. Writing unique, detailed product descriptions not only helps with SEO but also improves conversions.

Penguin Update (2012) – No More Spammy Links

Some store owners used to buy thousands of low-quality backlinks to boost rankings. Penguin cracked down on this, emphasizing the importance of earning high-quality, relevant links from authoritative sites. Instead of focusing on quantity, aim for backlinks from reputable sources like industry blogs, product review sites, or suppliers.

Mobile-First Indexing (2018-Present) – Mobile Optimization Is Essential

More than half of e-commerce traffic comes from mobile devices, and Google now prioritizes mobile-friendly websites. If your store isn't responsive, loads slowly, or has a poor mobile experience, your rankings will suffer. Tools like Google's Mobile-

Friendly Test can help you identify and fix issues.

Helpful Content Update (2022) – Prioritizing User Experience

Google now emphasizes content that is genuinely helpful rather than written just to rank. Product pages should be informative, engaging, and written with the customer in mind. If your content doesn't answer real questions or add value, it may not rank well, no matter how many keywords you include.

The Three Pillars of SEO: Technical, On-Page, and Off-Page

SEO is a broad discipline, but it can be broken down into three key areas: technical SEO, on-page SEO, and off-page SEO. Each pillar plays a critical role in improving your store's visibility.

Technical Seo: Optimizing The Foundation

Think of technical SEO as the behind-the-scenes work that makes your website easy for search engines to crawl and index. Even if you have great content, poor technical SEO can hold you back. Here are some essential elements:

Site Speed: A slow-loading site leads to higher bounce rates. Use tools like Google PageSpeed Insights to identify speed issues and optimize images, enable caching, and use a content delivery network (CDN).

Mobile Optimization: Since Google uses mobile-first indexing, your store must work flawlessly on smartphones and tablets.

Site Structure & URL Optimization: Clean, descriptive URLs (e.g., yoursite.com/mens-running-shoes) help search engines and users understand your pages better.

Schema Markup: This structured data helps search engines display rich results, like product ratings and prices, directly in search results.

On-Page Seo: Making Pages Search-Friendly

On-page SEO focuses on optimizing individual pages to rank higher. It includes:

Keyword Optimization: Using the right keywords in titles, product descriptions, and headings helps search engines match your page to relevant searches.

Product Descriptions: Avoid generic manufacturer descriptions. Write compelling, detailed descriptions that answer customer questions and naturally include keywords.

Title Tags & Meta Descriptions: These appear in search results and should be enticing enough to encourage clicks.

Internal Linking: Linking to related products or blog content improves navigation and helps distribute ranking power across your site.

Off-Page Seo: Building Authority & Trust

While technical and on-page SEO focus on improving your site, off-page SEO is about building its reputation. Google considers external factors like backlinks, social signals, and online mentions when determining rankings.

Backlink Building: Earning links from reputable sites tells Google your store is trustworthy. Strategies include guest blogging, PR outreach, and partnerships with influencers.

Social Media & Brand Mentions: While social signals don't directly impact rankings, a strong social presence can drive traffic and engagement, leading to more backlinks.

Customer Reviews: Positive reviews on Google, Trustpilot, and industry-specific platforms improve credibility and can boost local SEO.

***

Understanding how search engines work and applying SEO fundamentals is the first step to making your store more visible. Google's algorithms reward sites that offer a great user experience, valuable content, and technical optimization. While SEO takes time, focusing on these three pillars – technical, on-page, and off-page SEO – will help your store attract more customers and grow your business.

In the next chapters, we'll dive deeper into how

you can apply these strategies to your e-commerce store. From optimizing product pages to link-building techniques, you'll learn how to develop an SEO strategy that delivers lasting results.

KEYWORD RESEARCH FOR ONLINE STORES

When I first started working with online store owners, one of the biggest misconceptions I encountered was that simply listing products on their website would be enough to attract customers. They'd set up an e-commerce store, upload their inventory, and then wait for sales to roll in – only to be met with silence. The reality is, if your store isn't optimized for what people are searching for, it's like having a physical shop in the middle of nowhere with no signage. That's where keyword research comes in.

Understanding what your potential customers are typing into Google – and optimizing your store around those searches – is one of the most important aspects of e-commerce SEO. The right keywords can drive high-intent shoppers directly to your product pages, increasing conversions and sales. But not all keywords are created equal. Let's break down how to find the most valuable keywords for your online store and use them effectively.

Finding Buyer-Intent Keywords

vs. Informational Keywords

One of the first mistakes many e-commerce store owners make is targeting the wrong type of keywords. It's easy to go after broad, high-traffic keywords like "running shoes" or "handbags," but these often attract browsers rather than buyers. Instead, the most effective keywords are those with clear buyer intent – keywords that indicate the searcher is ready to make a purchase.

For example, let's say you sell organic skincare products. A keyword like "best face moisturizer" may get a lot of traffic, but it's more likely to attract people looking for general information. On the other hand, a keyword like "buy organic face moisturizer" or "organic face cream for dry skin" signals a strong intent to purchase. These are the terms you want to focus on because they bring in customers who are further along in the buying process.

Informational keywords, however, still have value. If you create blog content or buying guides, these keywords can help attract potential customers earlier in their journey. A blog post titled "How to Choose the Best Organic Moisturizer for Your Skin Type" might bring in readers who aren't ready to buy today, but they could become customers later. The key is to strategically use a mix of buyer-intent and informational keywords to capture customers at different stages of their journey.

Using Google Keyword Planner, Ahrefs, and Semrush

The good news is, you don't have to guess which keywords to use. There are powerful tools that can help you uncover the exact terms your potential customers are searching for. My top three go-to tools for keyword research are Google Keyword Planner, Ahrefs, and Semrush.

Google Keyword Planner is a great starting point, especially since it's free. By entering a keyword related to your product, you can see how many people search for it each month, how competitive it is, and get a list of related keywords. The trick here is to filter out keywords that are too broad and look for those with clear purchase intent.

Ahrefs is my favorite tool for a deeper dive. It not only shows search volume but also keyword difficulty, which helps you gauge how hard it will be to rank for a term. One of its best features is the ability to see what keywords your competitors are ranking for. We'll talk more about that later.

Semrush is another excellent tool with robust keyword analytics. It helps identify long-tail keyword opportunities and provides insights into what's working in your industry. One of my favorite features is the Keyword Magic Tool, which suggests thousands of related keyword ideas based on a seed keyword.

When using these tools, focus on keywords that have a balance of high search volume and low to medium competition. If a keyword has thousands of searches but is dominated by giant retailers like Amazon or Walmart, it will be tough to rank for. Instead, look for niche opportunities that align with what your store offers.

Long-Tail Keywords & How They Drive E-Commerce Sales

If I had to pick one SEO strategy that consistently delivers results for e-commerce stores, it would be targeting long-tail keywords. These are longer, more specific keyword phrases that may have lower search volume but higher conversion rates.

Let's go back to our skincare example. Instead of targeting "moisturizer," a long-tail keyword would be "best organic face moisturizer for sensitive skin." Fewer people search for this exact phrase, but those who do are highly likely to buy because it matches their specific needs.

Long-tail keywords are particularly valuable for e-commerce because they indicate strong purchase intent, they are easier to rank for compared to broad keywords, and they help you attract the right customers who are looking for exactly what you sell. Thought they don't have as much traffic individually, ranking for many long-tail keywords can generate as much traffic as a single broader keyword.

To find long-tail keywords, you can use Google's autocomplete feature (start typing a keyword in Google and see what suggestions appear). You can also look at the "People also ask" section in search results for common questions, or use tools like AnswerThePublic to find question-based searches related to your product.

One strategy I often recommend is incorporating long-tail keywords into your product descriptions, category pages, and blog content. Instead of just listing a product as "Face Moisturizer," optimize it for something more specific like "Hydrating Organic Face Moisturizer for Dry Skin - Paraben-Free." Not only does this help SEO, but it also improves click-through rates because it speaks directly to the customer's needs.

Competitor Keyword Analysis & Gap Opportunities

One of the smartest ways to refine your keyword strategy is to look at what's already working for your competitors. If another online store in your niche is ranking high in search results, they've likely done some of the heavy lifting in keyword research. By analyzing their keyword strategy, you can identify opportunities to outrank them or find gaps they've missed.

Using Ahrefs or Semrush, you can enter a competitor's domain and see which keywords they rank for, how much traffic they get from each keyword, and what keywords they are missing that you could capitalize on.

For example, let's say you sell handcrafted leather bags. You enter a competitor's site and discover that they rank highly for "handmade leather tote" but have no rankings for "handmade crossbody leather bag." This presents an opportunity to create optimized product pages and content around that gap.

Another effective strategy is reverse engineering their top-performing content. If they have a blog post titled "The Best Leather Bags for Travel" that's driving thousands of visitors, you could create an even better, more detailed version – perhaps "10 Best Leather Bags for Travel (With Expert Tips)."

This isn't about copying your competitors but learning from them and identifying areas where you can improve or differentiate your offerings.

***

Keyword research is the foundation of a successful e-commerce SEO strategy. By focusing on buyer-intent keywords, leveraging tools like Google Keyword Planner, Ahrefs, and Semrush, and targeting long-tail keywords, you can drive the right kind of traffic to your store. Competitive analysis helps you refine your approach and discover untapped opportunities.

The key takeaway? Don't just go after the biggest, most obvious keywords. Take the time to find the specific terms your customers are searching for –

because when you align your SEO with their intent, you won't just attract visitors, you'll attract buyers.

In the next chapter, we'll explore how to optimize your product pages to ensure all that great keyword research turns into real sales.

PART 2: ON-PAGE OPTIMIZATION FOR E-COMMERCE

OPTIMIZING PRODUCT PAGES FOR SEO

One of the most common mistakes I see in e-commerce SEO is underestimating the importance of product pages. Store owners spend time designing a beautiful website, driving traffic through ads, and even crafting great blog content – but when customers land on a product page, they're met with generic titles, thin descriptions, and poorly optimized images. This leads to missed sales and low search engine rankings.

Your product pages are the heart of your online store. They're where customers decide whether or not to make a purchase. And from an SEO perspective, they're also one of the most powerful tools for ranking in search results. If you optimize them correctly, you won't just attract visitors – you'll convert them into buyers. Let's dive into how to structure your product pages for both maximum search visibility and user engagement.

Writing Compelling Product Titles (Keywords + Clickability)

Think about the last time you searched for something online. Chances are, you clicked on a result that had a clear and compelling title that matched exactly what you were looking for. Your product titles should do the same for your customers.

A good product title balances SEO optimization and readability. That means including important keywords while also making it appealing for shoppers. Let's say you sell wireless earbuds. Instead of just labeling them "Wireless Earbuds," a better approach would be something like "Noise-Canceling Wireless Earbuds – Bluetooth 5.0 Headphones with 30-Hour Battery Life." This title is better because it includes important keywords like "noise-canceling," "wireless earbuds," and "Bluetooth 5.0," while also highlighting key selling points like battery life. Google can easily understand what the product is, and customers are more likely to click because they immediately see why this product might be better than others.

When crafting product titles, always put the most important keywords first, as Google places more weight on the beginning of a title. At the same time, keep it readable and natural – forcing too many keywords into a title makes it sound robotic. Including unique selling points such as battery life, material, brand name, or special features can make your product stand out. Formatting your titles in title case also improves readability and makes them look more professional.

Crafting SEO-Friendly Product Descriptions Without Keyword Stuffing

Product descriptions are where many store owners miss a huge SEO opportunity. A well-written description can increase conversions and improve rankings by providing valuable, keyword-rich content for search engines while answering questions for potential buyers.

One of the biggest mistakes I see is either too little content – just a few lines of generic text – or excessive keyword stuffing, where too many keywords are forced into the description. Neither approach works. A good product description should feel like a conversation with the customer – informative, engaging, and natural.

For example, if you were selling a memory foam pillow, a poor description might read, "Memory foam pillow, great for sleep, soft and comfortable, best pillow for sleeping." That doesn't tell the customer much, and it sounds robotic. Instead, a stronger description would be something like, "Get the best night's sleep with our premium memory foam pillow. Designed to contour to your head and neck, it provides optimal support and comfort. Made with cooling gel technology, it helps regulate temperature, so you stay cool throughout the night. Perfect for side and back sleepers looking for relief from neck pain." This version naturally includes keywords like "memory foam pillow," "cooling gel technology," and "relief from neck pain," but it also explains the product's benefits in a way that makes the reader want to buy.

When writing product descriptions, use natural language and write as if you were speaking directly to a customer. Highlight the benefits, not just the features. Instead of saying "100% cotton," explain that it's "soft, breathable cotton for all-day comfort." Anticipate customer questions and address them within the description. Focus on one or two primary keywords per description and use them naturally, ensuring they don't feel forced. Making descriptions easy to skim by using short paragraphs also improves readability and engagement.

Image Optimization: ALT Tags, File Names & Compression

High-quality images are essential for e-commerce, but they can also be a powerful SEO asset – if they are optimized correctly. Google can't "see" images the way humans do, so it relies on file names, ALT tags, and structured data to understand what an image is about.

Before uploading an image, renaming the file with descriptive keywords is crucial. Instead of something like IMG_12345.jpg, a more effective file name would be "wireless-earbuds-bluetooth-5.0-black.jpg." This helps search engines understand the image content and can improve rankings in Google

Image Search.

ALT tags are another important factor. They provide descriptions of images for visually impaired users and help search engines interpret image content. A generic ALT tag like "pillow" does little for SEO, whereas a more descriptive one like "Cooling memory foam pillow with breathable cover" improves accessibility and search visibility.

Compressing images is another important step, as large image files slow down page speed, which can negatively impact SEO and increase bounce rates. Using tools like TinyPNG or ShortPixel can help reduce file size without losing quality, ensuring that product pages load quickly and provide a smooth shopping experience.

Product Reviews & UGC for SEO (Why Google Loves Fresh Content)

One of the most underrated SEO strategies for product pages is leveraging customer reviews and user-generated content (UGC). Google loves fresh, unique content, and customer reviews provide exactly that. They help boost rankings, increase trust, and drive conversions.

Stores that encourage product reviews tend to rank higher because reviews add unique, keyword-rich content. Customers naturally include long-tail keywords in their feedback, which helps pages rank for additional search terms. Reviews also signal trust and credibility. Google favors stores with high engagement and positive reviews because they indicate a better user experience. On top of that, higher-rated products tend to get better click-through rates, as customers are more likely to purchase a product with a 4.8-star rating than one with no reviews.

To encourage more reviews, set up automatic emails that go out a few days after purchase, asking customers to share their experience. Offering small incentives, such as a discount code for leaving a review, can also increase participation. Make the review submission process as simple as possible to ensure more customers follow through.

Beyond text reviews, user-generated photos and videos are even more powerful. When customers upload pictures of themselves using your product, it adds authenticity and gives Google even more fresh content to crawl. Featuring these on product pages also builds social proof, helping to convince new visitors that your products are worth buying.

***

Optimizing your product pages is one of the most impactful things you can do for e-commerce SEO. A well-structured page that includes compelling product titles, engaging descriptions, optimized images, and user-generated reviews will not only rank higher in search results but also convert more visitors into customers. By paying attention to how your pages are crafted, you can create a better shopping experience while also gaining a competitive edge in search rankings.

In the next chapter, we'll dive into category pages and site architecture – two areas that can significantly improve your store's SEO when done right.

CATEGORY PAGES & SITE ARCHITECTURE

When I first started working with e-commerce stores, I noticed a pattern – many business owners focused all their SEO efforts on the homepage while completely neglecting their category pages. But here's the thing: category pages are some of the most powerful pages on an e-commerce site. They serve as a bridge between broad search queries and specific products, helping both customers and search engines understand the structure of your store. If optimized correctly, they can significantly improve your rankings, boost conversions, and enhance user experience.

The Role of Category Pages in SEO & Navigation

Category pages are more than just collections of products; they are key landing pages that help customers navigate your store efficiently. Imagine walking into a well-organized clothing store where jeans are in one section, jackets in another, and accessories in a separate space. Now, picture a store where everything is randomly piled up without labels or organization. Which one would you prefer? Search engines think the same way. A well-structured category page helps Google understand what your store is about and how products are grouped, improving your chances of ranking for broader, high-traffic search terms.

For example, if you sell running shoes, a properly optimized category page titled "Men's Running Shoes" could rank for terms like "best running shoes for men" or "lightweight running shoes." This means customers searching for general product categories – rather than specific brands or models – can find your store before they even know what specific product they want.

Beyond SEO, category pages play a crucial role in user experience. A well-designed category page allows shoppers to quickly browse through products, apply filters, and find what they need without frustration. If customers struggle to navigate your store, they're more likely to leave, increasing bounce rates and hurting your rankings.

How to Optimize Category Pages (URL Structure, Meta Data, Content)

A strong category page isn't just about displaying products; it needs to be optimized for search engines and users alike. One of the first areas to address is the URL structure. URLs should be clean, descriptive, and easy to understand. Instead of something messy like: yourstore.com/category? id=1234

A well-optimized URL would look like: yourstore.com/mens-running-shoes

This structure is more user-friendly and helps search engines understand the page's content.

Next, let's talk about meta titles and descriptions. These are what show up in search engine results, so they need to be compelling. A meta title for a category page should be both keyword-rich and engaging. Instead of just saying "Men's Running Shoes | XYZ Store," a stronger version would be: "Shop Men's Running Shoes – Lightweight & Supportive Styles | XYZ Store." This approach naturally includes important keywords while also appealing to potential customers.

The category page content itself is another overlooked opportunity. Many stores simply list products without any additional content, which is a wasted SEO chance. Adding a short, keyword-rich introduction at the top of the page can improve rankings and provide useful information to shoppers. For example, a category page for hiking backpacks might include a paragraph like:

"Explore our collection of durable and lightweight hiking backpacks, perfect for day hikes, overnight trips, and long expeditions. Designed with adjustable straps and weather-resistant materials, our top-rated backpacks ensure comfort and protection in any terrain."

This approach naturally incorporates keywords

while providing valuable information. Some stores also add an FAQ section below the product listings, answering common customer questions about sizing, materials, or care instructions. This not only improves user experience but also increases the page's keyword relevance.

Internal Linking Strategies to Pass Authority & Improve UX

Internal linking is one of the most effective ways to strengthen your category pages and help distribute SEO value throughout your store. If you've ever read a blog post that links to related articles or products, you've seen this in action. The goal is to create a web of connections between related content so that both users and search engines can easily navigate your site.

One best practice is to link from blog content to category pages. If you have a guide titled "How to Choose the Best Running Shoes for Your Foot Type", linking to your Men's Running Shoes and Women's Running Shoes category pages makes perfect sense. This not only improves SEO but also increases the chances of turning informational readers into buyers.

Another strategy is to use breadcrumb navigation, which is a secondary navigation system that helps users understand their location on your site. For example, a breadcrumb trail for a product page might look like:

Home > Men's Shoes > Running Shoes > Nike Air Zoom Pegasus 39

Breadcrumbs make it easier for shoppers to navigate back to category pages and also reinforce your site's structure for search engines, improving crawlability and rankings.

Finally, linking between related categories can help shoppers discover additional products. If someone is browsing your Winter Jackets category, a small block of text suggesting Hiking Boots or Thermal Gloves could keep them engaged longer, increasing the chances of additional sales.

Avoiding Thin Content & Duplicate Category Pages

As we discussed previously, one of the biggest mistakes e-commerce stores make with category pages is thin content – pages that contain little more than a list of products and no additional information. Equally as problematic are duplicate category pages, which can occur when variations of the same category exist under different URLs. For example, if your store has pages like:

yourstore.com/mens-running-shoes

yourstore.com/mens-footwear/running-shoes

yourstore.com/running/mens-shoes

Search engines may see these as separate pages competing for the same keyword, which can dilute rankings. To fix this, use canonical tags to tell Google which version of the page is the primary one, preventing duplicate content issues.

Another common mistake is creating separate category pages for every minor product variation. Instead of having different categories for Red Running Shoes, Blue Running Shoes, and Black Running Shoes, it's better to have one optimized Running Shoes category with color filter options. This keeps the site clean, prevents unnecessary duplication, and improves SEO.

***

Category pages are more than just product collections – they are essential tools for both SEO and user experience. When optimized correctly, they help search engines understand your site structure, make navigation easier for customers, and improve your chances of ranking for high-traffic keywords. Focusing on clean URL structures, engaging meta data, well-written category descriptions, and strategic internal linking can make a huge difference in how well these pages perform.

In the next chapter, we'll explore technical SEO strategies that can further enhance your store's crawlability, speed, and overall ranking potential.

TECHNICAL SEO FOR E-COMMERCE SITES

Many store owners are surprised to learn that technical SEO can make or break their rankings. While optimizing product and category pages is essential, search engines also need to be able to crawl, understand, and trust your website. If your store is slow, difficult to navigate, or filled with duplicate content, even the best keyword strategy won't get you far. Technical SEO ensures that your site functions smoothly for both search engines and customers, leading to better rankings and higher conversions.

Improving Site Speed & Core Web Vitals

Speed is everything in e-commerce. If your site takes too long to load, customers will leave before they even see your products. Google also takes site speed seriously – its Core Web Vitals update prioritizes fast-loading, smooth-functioning websites. If your store doesn't meet these standards, it's going to struggle in search rankings.

One of the first things I do when auditing an e-commerce site is run it through Google PageSpeed

Insights. This tool reveals how quickly pages load and provides recommendations for improvement. If your store is slow, the culprits are often large image files, too many scripts, or poor server performance.

Optimizing images is one of the easiest and most effective fixes. I've worked with stores that had massive product images – several megabytes in size – slowing down their load times. By compressing images using tools like TinyPNG or ShortPixel, they instantly saw an improvement in speed without sacrificing quality. Additionally, using next-gen image formats like WebP instead of PNG or JPEG can further reduce file sizes while maintaining clarity.

Another common issue is excessive JavaScript and CSS slowing down a site. If your homepage has unnecessary animations, pop-ups, and third-party tracking scripts, they could be dragging down performance. Minifying CSS and JavaScript files and using lazy loading for images and videos can help keep things running smoothly. If you're using a platform like Shopify or BigCommerce, check for any unnecessary apps or plugins – sometimes, less is more.

Your web hosting also plays a huge role. A cheap, shared hosting plan might work for a small blog, but for e-commerce, you need a fast, reliable hosting provider. If your store is growing, consider using a Content Delivery Network (CDN) like Cloudflare or Amazon CloudFront to serve pages more efficiently to customers around the world.

Mobile Optimization & Mobile-First Indexing

You've probably seen in your own life over the last few years that more and more people are shopping from their phones instead of desktop computers. Google caught onto this trend and introduced mobile-first indexing, meaning it primarily evaluates the mobile version of a website when determining rankings. If your store isn't mobile-friendly, you're missing out on both traffic and sales.

The first step in mobile optimization is ensuring your website is responsive, meaning it adapts your layouts to different screen sizes. If your text is too small, buttons are hard to tap, or images don't scale properly, shoppers will get frustrated and leave.

Navigation is another critical factor. A desktop menu with multiple dropdowns might work fine, but on mobile, it can become overwhelming. Simplify navigation by using a hamburger menu, prioritizing key categories, and making search functionality easy to find.

Site speed is even more crucial on mobile. Mobile users often browse or buy while they're on the go. This means they may be connected via wifi or a cellular network which is slower than a home or office internet connection. Because of this, a slow-loading site can be a dealbreaker for mobile shoppers.

Checkout optimization is another area that often gets overlooked. If your mobile checkout process is too complicated, you'll lose customers at the final step. Offering one-click checkout options like Apple Pay, Google Pay, or Shop Pay can significantly improve mobile conversion rates. I've seen stores significantly improve their mobile conversions simply by adding digital wallet payment options to their checkout.

Canonical Tags & Handling Duplicate Content Issues

Duplicate content is one of the biggest SEO challenges in e-commerce. Unlike blogs or service-based websites, online stores often have multiple product variations, similar product descriptions, and category pages that create unintended duplicates. If search engines see too many similar pages, they might struggle to determine which one to rank – or worse, penalize your site for duplicate content.

One of the best ways to prevent this issue is by using canonical tags. A canonical tag is a simple piece of code that tells search engines which version of a page is the "main" one. For example, if you have multiple URLs leading to the same product due to different filter options, you can set a canonical tag pointing to the preferred URL. This prevents dilution of ranking signals and ensures that the correct page gets indexed.

I've seen e-commerce sites that had hundreds of product pages with minor variations (like color or size), all competing against each other in search rankings. By implementing canonical tags and consolidating similar pages, you can clean up their SEO and improve rankings without sacrificing customer experience.

Another common duplicate content issue happens when stores copy manufacturer descriptions for their products. If dozens of other stores are using the same text, your pages won't stand out. Writing unique, detailed product descriptions not only improves SEO but also makes your products more appealing to customers. If it's too time-consuming to write unique descriptions for every product, focus on items that have the highest search volume or profit.

XML Sitemaps & Robots.txt for E-Commerce Stores

Search engines rely on XML sitemaps to understand the structure of your website and discover important pages. An XML sitemap acts like a roadmap, guiding search engines to your most important content. Without one, some of your key product pages might not get indexed, which means they won't appear in search results.

For e-commerce stores, it's crucial to have a well-structured sitemap that includes product pages, category pages, and any important landing pages. If you're using Shopify, BigCommerce, or WooCommerce, your platform likely generates a sitemap automatically, but you should still check it in Google Search Console to ensure all critical pages are included. You can submit secondary sitemaps if you discover some pages are missing from the dynamic version generated by your platform.

Equally important is the robots.txt file, which tells search engines which pages they should or shouldn't crawl. This is especially useful for preventing search engines from indexing duplicate pages, such as those created by filtering and sorting options. However, misusing the robots.txt file can be dangerous – blocking the wrong pages can result in Google ignoring important parts of your site. I've seen clients block product pages by accident, which completely removed them from search results.

Regularly checking your Google Search Console Crawl Errors can help ensure search engines are indexing the right pages and not running into roadblocks.

***

Technical SEO might not be as flashy as content marketing or link building, but it's absolutely essential for e-commerce success. A slow-loading, unstructured, or duplicate-filled website will struggle to rank no matter how great the content is. By improving site speed, ensuring mobile optimization, fixing duplicate content issues, and managing sitemaps and robots.txt correctly, you'll create a solid technical foundation that allows your store to rank higher and convert more visitors into customers.

In the next chapter, we'll dive into structured data and rich snippets – powerful tools that can make your product listings stand out in search results and attract even more clicks.

PART 3: ADVANCED SEO STRATEGIES FOR E-COMMERCE

STRUCTURED DATA & RICH SNIPPETS

One of the most important parts of e-commerce SEO is structured data. When I first started optimizing online stores, I realized that even though my clients had great products, their search listings looked plain and unremarkable compared to competitors. This all changed with the introduction of rich snippets, which display reviews, prices and other product details directly in search results. If you want your store to attract more clicks, structured data is a must-have.

Understanding Schema Markup for E-Commerce

Structured data, also known as schema markup, is a way of organizing and labeling information on your website so that search engines can better understand it. Instead of just guessing what your page is about, Google can read the structured data and display richer, more informative search results.

For e-commerce, this means that when a customer searches for a product you sell, your listing can show additional details like price, availability, brand, and customer ratings. These enhanced search results, known as rich snippets, help improve click-through rates because they provide useful information upfront, making your listing more appealing compared to competitors with standard results.

Implementing schema markup isn't just about making your search results look good; it also helps search engines categorize your content more accurately. This leads to better indexing and can improve your rankings. Google favors pages that provide structured, well-organized information, so using schema markup gives your store a competitive edge.

Implementing Product Schema for Enhanced Listings

One of the most important types of schema markup for e-commerce is Product Schema. This tells Google the key details of your product, such as:

Product name
Description
Price and currency
Availability (in stock, out of stock, pre-order)
Brand
SKU
Review ratings

By adding this structured data to your product

pages, you increase the chances of your product appearing in Google's rich results, which means more visibility and higher click-through rates. Let's say you're selling a stainless steel French press coffee maker. Without schema markup, your search result would be just a standard link with a meta description. But with Product Schema, your search result could include the star rating, price, and whether it's in stock – giving customers more information right away and making them more likely to click on your listing.

Most major e-commerce platforms, like Shopify and WooCommerce, offer built-in options or apps/plugins to implement structured data. If you're using a custom-built store, you might need to manually add JSON-LD structured data to your product pages. JSON-LD (JavaScript Object Notation for Linked Data) is Google's preferred format because it's easy to implement and doesn't interfere with your website's content.

Using FAQ & Review Schema to Improve Click-Through Rates

Beyond product schema, other types of structured data can further enhance your store's search results. Two of the most useful for e-commerce sites are FAQ Schema and Review Schema.

FAQ Schema allows you to display frequently asked questions directly in search results. Imagine a customer searches for "how to clean a leather wallet" and your store has a product page for a leather care kit. If you've added FAQ Schema with answers to common cleaning questions, Google may display these directly in the search results. This provides immediate value to searchers and increases the chances they'll click through to your page.

Similarly, Review Schema helps highlight customer ratings and testimonials. If a product has dozens of five-star reviews, why not showcase that in search results? Customers are more likely to trust and click on listings with strong social proof. Google's algorithm also recognizes review-rich pages as more credible, which can indirectly improve your rankings.

By implementing both FAQ and Review Schema, you create a richer search presence, attract more clicks, and provide valuable information before the customer even visits your site.

Testing & Debugging Structured Data with Google Tools

One of the biggest concerns I hear from store owners is whether they've implemented structured data correctly. If your schema markup has errors, Google may ignore it or, worse, misinterpret your content. Thankfully, Google provides free tools to test and debug structured data.

The first tool I always recommend is Google's

Rich Results Test. This tool lets you enter a product page URL and see exactly how Google interprets the structured data. It also flags any errors or missing fields, so you can make adjustments before your page goes live.

Another essential tool is Google Search Console. Once you implement structured data, you can monitor how Google is using it in search results. If there are issues, Google will notify you so you can fix them promptly. This is especially useful for e-commerce stores with a large number of product pages.

If you're comfortable with technical SEO, you can also check your schema markup manually using Google's Structured Data Testing Tool or Schema.org's Markup Validator. These tools let you paste in raw JSON-LD code and see if it's formatted correctly. For non-technical store owners, I usually recommend working with an SEO expert or using an automated schema plugin to ensure everything is set up properly.

***

Structured data and rich snippets can transform how your products appear in search results, making them more informative and attractive to potential buyers. By implementing Product Schema, FAQ Schema, and Review Schema, you can enhance your search listings, improve click-through rates, and even boost your overall SEO performance.

Getting structured data right takes a little effort,

but the payoff is huge. Customers are more likely to click on search results that provide useful details upfront, and Google rewards well-structured pages with better visibility. If you haven't already added schema markup to your store, now is the time to start.

In the next chapter, we'll dive into link-building strategies for e-commerce stores – how to earn high-quality backlinks and establish your site as an authority in your niche.

LINK BUILDING & OFF-PAGE SEO

When I first started working with e-commerce clients, I quickly learned that even the best on-page SEO won't get you far without strong off-page signals. Google doesn't just look at your store's content – it also considers how many other reputable sites link to it. If search engines see that high-quality, trusted websites are linking to your store, they view it as an authority, which can significantly boost your rankings. This is why link building is one of the most powerful strategies in e-commerce SEO.

Unlike on-page SEO, where you have full control, link building requires outreach, networking, and sometimes a bit of creativity. However, when done right, it helps drive more organic traffic, improves credibility, and increases brand visibility. Let's break down how backlinks impact SEO and how you can earn high-quality links for your online store.

How Backlinks Impact E-Commerce SEO

Backlinks, or inbound links, are links from other websites that point to your store. Think of them as votes of confidence. When a well-respected website links to your store, Google interprets it as a sign that your site is trustworthy and valuable. The more high-quality backlinks you have, the better your chances of ranking higher in search results.

However, not all backlinks are created equal. A link from a reputable news site, a popular industry blog, or a well-known supplier is far more valuable than a link from a random, low-quality directory. In fact, low-quality backlinks can actually harm your rankings, especially if they come from spammy or irrelevant sources.

One of the most common mistakes store owners make is assuming that link building means buying links. Google strictly forbids paid link schemes, and if it catches you, your site could be penalized. Instead, focus on earning backlinks naturally through valuable content, partnerships, and strategic outreach.

Guest Posting & Digital PR for E-Commerce

One of the most effective ways to build high-quality backlinks is through guest posting and digital PR. Guest posting involves writing articles for industry-related blogs, while digital PR focuses on getting featured in news articles, product roundups, and online magazines.

Guest posting works because it allows you to provide value to another website's audience while earning a backlink in return. For example, if you run an online store selling eco-friendly home products, you could write a guest post for a sustainability blog about "10 Simple Ways to Reduce Waste at Home." Within the article, you can naturally link back to a relevant product page on your store.

To get started with guest posting, make a list of blogs in your niche and reach out with topic ideas that align with their audience. Most websites are open to guest contributions as long as the content is valuable and well-written.

Digital PR, on the other hand, is about getting featured in major publications. This could be in the form of a product review, a feature in a gift guide, or a mention in a trending news article. One was to do this is by joining a service called Qwoted, where journalists look for expert sources to quote in their articles. If you can position yourself as an expert in your industry, you might land a mention in a high-authority publication like Forbes or Business Insider.

Getting High-Quality Links from Suppliers & Partners

One of the easiest yet most overlooked ways to get backlinks is by leveraging relationships with your suppliers, manufacturers, and business partners. If you sell products from well-known brands, check if they have a "Where to Buy" or "Retailers" page on their website. Many suppliers list their authorized resellers and link back to their stores. Getting your store included in these lists not only provides a valuable backlink but also helps drive targeted traffic from customers looking for specific brands.

Beyond suppliers, think about partnerships. If you collaborate with influencers, wholesale buyers, or even other e-commerce businesses, there may be opportunities to exchange links in a way that benefits both parties. For example, if you sell artisanal coffee and partner with a company that makes sustainable coffee mugs, you could feature each other's products on your blogs and exchange links.

Another strategy is to contribute testimonials for tools or services you use. If you've had a great experience with an e-commerce platform, a payment processor, or a marketing agency, offering a testimonial might earn you a backlink from their website. Many companies showcase customer testimonials and include a link to the business's site.

Leveraging Affiliate & Influencer Marketing for SEO

Affiliate marketing and influencer collaborations can also play a role in link building. When influencers or affiliate partners promote your products, they often link back to your store. While some of these links may be "nofollow" (meaning they don't pass SEO authority), they still help drive traffic and increase brand awareness. Additionally, if a high-authority website picks up your product because it was featured by an influencer, that could lead to valuable "dofollow" backlinks over time.

When choosing influencers or bloggers to work with, prioritize those with a strong domain authority and a relevant audience. If you sell fitness gear, collaborating with a well-known fitness blogger will be far more beneficial than working with a general lifestyle influencer who doesn't specialize in your niche.

In addition to influencers, affiliate programs can help scale your link-building efforts. When affiliates promote your products through their blogs, review sites, or social media, they create natural backlinks to your store. While these links are often tagged as affiliate links, search engines still recognize the traffic and engagement they generate, which can contribute to your overall SEO strength.

***

Link building is a crucial component of off-page SEO that can significantly impact your e-commerce store's search rankings. By focusing on earning high-quality backlinks through guest posting, digital PR, supplier relationships, and influencer partnerships, you can build a strong foundation of trust and authority in your industry.

It's important to remember that link building is a long-term strategy. Unlike on-page SEO changes, which can have immediate effects, building a network of quality backlinks takes time. However, the effort is worth it – strong backlinks not only improve search rankings but also drive referral traffic and enhance your brand's credibility.

In the next chapter, we'll explore content marketing for e-commerce SEO, including how to create compelling blog content, buying guides, and video strategies that attract and convert customers.

CONTENT MARKETING FOR E-COMMERCE SEO

When I first started working with e-commerce businesses, I often encountered store owners who were skeptical about content marketing. "Why do I need a blog if I'm selling products?" they'd ask. The reality is, content is one of the most powerful ways to drive organic traffic, build trust with potential customers, and establish your store as an authority in your niche. Search engines love fresh, relevant content, and a well-executed content marketing strategy can make a massive difference in how visible your store is online.

Blogging for E-Commerce (How to Drive Organic Traffic)

Many e-commerce store owners overlook blogging because they assume customers only visit their site to buy, not to read. However, the truth is that a blog can serve as a powerful traffic engine, attracting potential buyers at different stages of their purchasing journey. Some visitors may be in the early research phase, looking for advice on what product to buy, while others are ready to purchase but need a final push.

A great example of this is an online store selling camping gear. Instead of just listing products, a well-maintained blog could include articles like "The Best Tents for Winter Camping," "How to Choose the Right Sleeping Bag for Your Trip," or "5 Essential Camping Gadgets You Didn't Know You Needed." These posts naturally attract users searching for those topics on Google, bringing in traffic that might not have otherwise discovered your store.

When writing blog content, the key is to focus on providing value first and selling second. Blog posts should educate and solve customer problems, not just push products. However, you can naturally weave in product recommendations by linking to relevant items in your store. If someone is reading a post about "How to Choose the Best Running Shoes," they are likely in the market for running shoes – so including internal links to your top-selling models makes perfect sense.

Creating SEO-Optimized Buying Guides & Comparison Pages

One of the most effective content strategies for e-commerce stores is creating in-depth buying guides and product comparison pages. These types of pages rank exceptionally well in search results because they answer the exact questions shoppers are asking before making a purchase.

A buying guide helps customers navigate their choices by breaking down different product features, use cases, and key considerations. If you sell kitchen appliances, for example, a guide titled "How to Choose the Best Espresso Machine for Your Home" could cover various machine types, budget ranges, and features, while strategically linking to different models you sell.

Comparison pages, on the other hand, are perfect for shoppers trying to decide between multiple products. People often search for direct comparisons like "iPhone vs. Samsung Galaxy" or "Best DSLR Camera Under $1000." If your store sells tech gadgets, a well-structured comparison page highlighting the pros and cons of different models can attract high-intent buyers who are on the verge of making a decision. One of my clients recently implemented comprehensive product comparison pages and some of them are now in his top 10 landing pages for SEO traffic.

To optimize these pages for SEO, it's important to use long-tail keywords that match user intent. Instead of just targeting "best espresso machine," a better approach would be "best espresso machine for beginners" or "best espresso machine under $500." These long-tail phrases have lower competition and attract buyers looking for specific recommendations.

Video SEO for E-Commerce (YouTube,

Product Demos & Tutorials)

Video content is becoming increasingly important for SEO, especially in e-commerce. Google often features video results at the top of search pages, and YouTube itself is the second-largest search engine in the world. If you're not incorporating video into your content strategy, you're missing out on a major opportunity to drive traffic and increase conversions.

Product demonstration videos are one of the most effective types of video content for e-commerce. A customer might hesitate to buy a product just by looking at static images, but a well-made demo video showing the product in action can remove uncertainty and boost confidence. For example, if you sell fitness equipment, a video showcasing how to properly use a resistance band or a home treadmill can provide valuable insight while subtly encouraging the purchase.

Another powerful approach is creating how-to and tutorial videos that answer common customer questions. If your store sells skincare products, a video titled "How to Build a Skincare Routine for Acne-Prone Skin" could attract thousands of potential customers searching for skincare advice. Throughout the video, you can highlight your products as solutions to their needs.

To optimize videos for SEO, make sure to use relevant keywords in your video title, description, and tags. If you upload videos to YouTube, include a detailed description with timestamps, a clear call-to-action, and links back to your product pages. Embedding videos on your e-commerce site can also improve on-page engagement, keeping visitors on your site longer – a factor Google considers when ranking pages.

The Role of AI-Generated Content (Best Practices & Warnings)

With the rise of AI-powered writing tools, many e-commerce store owners are exploring automated content generation to save time. AI can be an excellent tool for brainstorming content ideas, generating product descriptions, or drafting initial blog posts. However, it's crucial to understand both its benefits and limitations.

One of the main advantages of AI-generated content is speed. If you need to create a large volume of product descriptions quickly, AI can provide a good starting point. However, these descriptions should always be reviewed and edited by a human to ensure they sound natural, engaging, and aligned with your brand's voice. Search engines prioritize high-quality, original content, so simply copying and pasting AI-generated text without refinement could hurt your rankings.

Another area where AI can be helpful is summarizing data and creating structured content, such as product comparisons or FAQs. However, AI-generated articles should be fact-checked, as these tools sometimes generate inaccurate or outdated information. Google has made it clear that while AI-written content isn't inherently bad, low-quality AI-generated text designed purely to manipulate rankings will be penalized.

To make the most of AI, I recommend using it as an assistant rather than a replacement. Use it to brainstorm ideas or for generating drafts, but add a personal touch, expert insights, and engaging storytelling to make the content valuable for both search engines and customers.

***

Content marketing is one of the most effective ways to drive organic traffic and establish your store as a trusted resource in your niche. Blogging, buying guides, comparison pages, and video content all work together to attract potential customers, answer their questions, and guide them toward making a purchase. When done correctly, content marketing not only improves SEO but also enhances customer trust and loyalty.

The key takeaway is that content should always provide value first. Instead of focusing solely on selling, aim to educate and engage your audience. If your content genuinely helps customers, they'll be more likely to buy from you – and search engines will reward you with higher rankings.

In the next chapter, we'll dive into SEO analytics and performance monitoring – how to track your progress, measure success, and refine your strategy to keep improving over time.

PART 4: TRACKING & MEASURING SEO SUCCESS

SEO ANALYTICS & PERFORMANCE MONITORING

One of the most common mistakes I see among e-commerce store owners is a desire to "do" SEO once and then be done with it. The reality is, SEO is an ongoing process, and the only way to know if your efforts are paying off is by tracking and analyzing your performance. Understanding SEO analytics isn't just about looking at traffic numbers – it's about identifying which strategies are working, which ones need improvement, and how visitors are interacting with your site.

I always tell clients that SEO isn't just about ranking on Google; it's about getting the right traffic and converting that traffic into customers. In this chapter, I'll walk you through how to set up essential tracking tools, monitor key performance indicators, and use data to refine your SEO strategy over time.

Setting Up Google Search Console & Google Analytics 4

Before diving into performance analysis, you

need to have the right tools in place. The two most essential tools for SEO tracking are Google Search Console (GSC) and Google Analytics 4 (GA4). These tools provide invaluable insights into how your website is performing in search results and how users behave once they land on your site.

Google Search Console is specifically designed to help website owners understand how their site appears in Google search results. Once you set it up and verify ownership of your website, you'll be able to track important metrics like search impressions, clicks, and keyword rankings. One of my favorite features in GSC is the Performance Report, which shows you exactly which queries are driving traffic to your store. If you notice that certain product pages are getting impressions but not clicks, it might be a sign that you need to improve your meta titles and descriptions to make them more compelling.

Google Analytics 4, on the other hand, gives you deeper insights into how users interact with your site. It helps answer key questions like:

Where is my traffic coming from?

How long are visitors staying on my pages?

Which pages are driving conversions?

Unlike older versions of Google Analytics, GA4 uses an event-based tracking system, which provides a more detailed view of user interactions. Setting up conversion tracking is crucial for e-commerce stores because it allows you to measure actions like product purchases, cart additions, and form submissions. Without this data, you won't know whether your SEO efforts are translating into actual revenue.

Tracking Rankings & Organic Traffic

Once your tracking tools are set up, the next step is monitoring your organic traffic and keyword rankings. Many store owners focus only on rankings, but I always stress that rankings alone don't tell the full story. What really matters is whether those rankings are driving high-quality traffic that converts.

To track keyword rankings, you can use Google Search Console, which provides a list of keywords your site is ranking for, along with their average positions. However, for more advanced tracking, third-party tools like Ahrefs, SEMrush, or Moz are incredibly useful. These tools allow you to track your rankings over time, compare them to competitors, and identify opportunities to target new keywords.

When analyzing rankings, one important thing to remember is search intent. If a page ranks well but isn't driving conversions, you may be targeting the wrong type of keyword. For example, ranking #1 for an informational keyword like "how to clean suede shoes" is great, but if your goal is to sell suede cleaner, you need to ensure your content also targets transactional keywords like "buy suede shoe cleaner."

Organic traffic should also be evaluated alongside engagement metrics. If you notice a spike in traffic but a low conversion rate, it could mean that visitors aren't finding what they expected. This is where deeper performance monitoring comes into play.

Monitoring CTRs, Bounce Rates, and Conversion Rates

Ranking high in search results is just the first step – getting users to click on your listing and engage with your site is just as important. Three key metrics to pay attention to are Click-Through Rate (CTR), Bounce Rate, and Conversion Rate.

Click-Through Rate (CTR) measures how often people click on your site when they see it in search results. If you have a low CTR, it means your title and meta description may not be compelling enough. A quick fix is to rewrite your meta descriptions to include power words, numbers, or a clear call-to-action. For example, instead of "Shop our latest running shoes", try "Best-Selling Running Shoes – Free Shipping & 20% Off Today!"

Bounce Rate refers to the percentage of visitors who leave your site after viewing just one page. A high bounce rate might indicate that your content isn't meeting user expectations or that your site's loading speed is too slow. If visitors land on a product page but immediately leave, consider whether the page provides enough valuable content, clear navigation, and compelling visuals to keep them engaged. In addition, make sure your meta tags are accurate so you're setting the right expectations for visitors.

Conversion Rate is arguably the most important metric for e-commerce SEO. You could have thousands of visitors, but if none of them are making purchases, something is off. I always recommend testing different product page layouts, pricing strategies, and call-to-action buttons to see what resonates best with your audience. If needed, you can run A/B tests to experiment with different elements on your site and measure what leads to more sales.

Using Heatmaps & User Behavior Analytics

One of the most underrated tools for improving SEO and user experience is heatmap tracking. Heatmaps visually show where users click, scroll, and spend the most time on your site. I've had clients who assumed their product pages were perfectly optimized, only to discover through heatmap analysis that users weren't even scrolling past the first section.

Heatmap tools like Hotjar and Lucky Orange can reveal a lot about how customers interact with your site. If you see that users are frequently abandoning their carts at a certain point, there may be a problem with your checkout process. If they're not clicking on important buttons, you may need to adjust your page layout or add stronger calls to action.

Another useful feature in these tools is session recordings, which allow you to watch real users navigate your site. This can highlight frustrating bottlenecks, confusing navigation, or broken elements that might be driving potential customers away.

**

SEO isn't just about optimizing your site and hoping for the best – it's about constantly measuring, refining, and improving based on real data. By setting up Google Search Console and Google Analytics 4, tracking rankings and organic traffic, monitoring engagement metrics, and using heatmaps to analyze user behavior, you can make data-driven decisions that lead to better SEO results.

The key takeaway here is that SEO is a continuous process. What works today might not work six months from now, and staying on top of performance metrics allows you to adapt your strategy accordingly. With the right tracking and analysis in place, you'll not only improve your search rankings but also increase your store's conversions and revenue.

In the next chapter, we'll explore common SEO mistakes that e-commerce store owners make and how to fix them, so you can avoid costly errors and keep your rankings moving in the right direction.

COMMON SEO MISTAKES & HOW TO FIX THEM

Over the years, I've seen a recurring theme: store owners would implement a few basic SEO tactics, see minimal results, and then assume that SEO simply didn't work for them. But more often than not, the real problem wasn't the strategy itself – it was the hidden mistakes they didn't even realize they were making.

SEO is a powerful long-term investment, but if you're unknowingly making mistakes, it can feel like you're running on a treadmill – working hard but getting nowhere. In this chapter, I'll walk you through some of the most common SEO mistakes I've seen in e-commerce and, more importantly, how to fix them.

Keyword Cannibalization

One of the most overlooked SEO mistakes in e-commerce is keyword cannibalization – when multiple pages on your site compete for the same keyword. While it might seem logical to target the same keyword across multiple product pages or blog posts, doing so can actually hurt your rankings.

Instead of strengthening your SEO, you end up confusing Google about which page to rank, and your pages end up competing against each other.

For example, let's say you sell handmade leather wallets, and you have five different product pages all optimized for the keyword "best leather wallet." Instead of one strong page ranking highly, Google might split the ranking authority among all five, causing none of them to reach the first page.

You need to consolidate and prioritize. If you have multiple pages targeting the same keyword, identify the most authoritative or highest-converting page and optimize it fully. The other pages can be modified to target more specific, long-tail variations, such as "best leather wallet for men" or "handmade brown leather wallet." You can also use internal linking to point from the less important pages to the main one, signaling to Google which page is the most valuable.

If keyword cannibalization is an issue across your site, tools like Ahrefs, SEMrush, or Google Search Console can help identify overlapping keywords and pages competing for the same terms.

Ignoring Technical SEO Issues

I've seen so many e-commerce businesses pour all their effort into keywords and content, only to neglect the technical foundation of their website. The problem is, without solid technical SEO, even the best content won't rank well.

Some of the most common technical SEO issues include slow site speed, broken links, duplicate content, improper use of canonical tags, and poor mobile optimization. Google prioritizes websites that offer a smooth user experience, and technical flaws can drag down your rankings without you even realizing it.

One of the easiest ways to check your site's technical health is by running an audit using Google Search Console, Screaming Frog, or SEMrush's Site Audit tool. These tools will flag broken links, duplicate content, and other hidden issues.

One critical mistake I often see is ignoring mobile optimization. Since Google now uses mobile-first indexing, your site needs to work perfectly on mobile devices. This is true even if your typical customer isn't shopping on a mobile device. If your store isn't responsive or takes too long to load on a phone, your rankings will suffer.

If your site speed is slow, image optimization, lazy loading, and caching can make a huge difference. Large product images often slow down e-commerce sites, so compressing them with tools like TinyPNG or ShortPixel can improve loading times without sacrificing quality.

Over-Reliance on Paid Traffic Without SEO Strategy

I've worked with many store owners who get stuck in a cycle of spending thousands on paid ads but ignoring their organic traffic strategy. While paid traffic can deliver quick results, it's not sustainable in the long run if you don't invest in SEO. The moment you stop paying for ads, the traffic disappears.

Relying too much on Google Ads, Facebook Ads, or influencer marketing without an SEO strategy is like renting traffic instead of owning it. The goal of SEO is to build a steady stream of organic visitors who find your store naturally through search engines – without the ongoing costs of advertising.

If your current strategy depends heavily on paid traffic, start by allocating some resources toward content marketing and keyword optimization. Creating valuable blog posts, buying guides, and product comparison pages can help attract organic traffic over time.

Another overlooked benefit of SEO is that it helps improve your Quality Score for paid ads. Google rewards websites with strong SEO by charging them lower costs per click (CPC) in Google Ads. So by improving your site speed, mobile-friendliness, and keyword relevance, you can actually reduce your paid advertising costs while boosting your organic rankings.

The best approach is to strike a balance between paid and organic traffic. Use ads for quick wins, but also invest in long-term SEO strategies that will bring in consistent traffic without requiring ongoing ad spend.

Recovering from a Google Penalty

Few things are scarier for an e-commerce store than getting hit with a Google penalty. If your rankings suddenly drop overnight, it could be a sign that Google has flagged your site for violating its guidelines.

There are two main types of penalties: manual penalties and algorithmic penalties. Manual penalties occur when a Google reviewer determines that your site has violated their policies, while algorithmic penalties happen automatically due to updates in Google's ranking algorithms.

The first step in recovering from a penalty is identifying what caused it. Google Search Console will notify you if your site has received a manual penalty, often due to issues like spammy backlinks or thin content. If this happens, you'll need to fix the problem and submit a reconsideration request to Google.

Algorithmic penalties, on the other hand, are harder to diagnose. If your rankings drop after a major Google update, check resources like Moz's Google Algorithm Update History to see if a new update has affected sites in your industry.

The best way to recover from a penalty is to clean up any low-quality backlinks, remove duplicate or thin content, and ensure your site follows Google's best practices. If you've previously engaged in shady link-building tactics or keyword stuffing, now is the time to fix those issues and focus on high-quality, user-friendly content.

***

SEO mistakes are more common than most store owners realize, but the good news is that they're fixable. By addressing keyword cannibalization, improving your site's technical SEO, balancing paid traffic with organic growth, and steering clear of Google penalties, you'll build a stronger foundation for long-term search visibility.

The biggest lesson I've learned over the years is that SEO isn't about quick wins – it's about creating a foundation for sustainable growth. The stores that succeed in organic search aren't necessarily the ones with the biggest budgets, but the ones that consistently optimize, analyze, and improve over time.

In the next chapter, we'll look at how to future-proof your e-commerce SEO strategy, ensuring that your store continues to rank well even as search algorithms evolve and new trends emerge.

PART 5: FUTURE-PROOFING YOUR E-COMMERCE SEO

THE FUTURE OF SEO IN E-COMMERCE

SEO is constantly evolving, and nowhere is this more evident than in e-commerce. Over the years, I've seen firsthand how changes in search algorithms, emerging technologies, and shifting consumer behaviors have reshaped the way online stores compete for visibility. What worked five years ago is no longer enough, and the strategies that will drive success in the next five years are already taking shape.

The good news is that if you stay ahead of these trends, you can outpace competitors who are slow to adapt. The bad news? SEO isn't something you can set and forget – it requires continuous learning, testing, and refinement. In this chapter, I'll explore some of the most significant developments shaping the future of SEO and how you can position your e-commerce store for long-term success.

AI & Machine Learning in Search Algorithms

One of the most transformative changes in search

engines over the past decade has been the rise of artificial intelligence (AI) and machine learning. Google's search algorithms are no longer based purely on keyword matching – they're powered by AI models that continuously learn and adapt to deliver the most relevant results.

Take Google's RankBrain, for example. Introduced in 2015, RankBrain is an AI system that helps Google process and understand search queries more like a human. Instead of just matching keywords, it analyzes the intent behind a search and ranks results accordingly. This means that keyword stuffing and rigid SEO tactics are no longer effective. Instead, the focus needs to be on creating high-quality, relevant content that truly answers a user's search intent.

Another AI-driven update is Google's Helpful Content Update, which prioritizes original, user-focused content over pages created just to manipulate rankings. E-commerce stores that rely on thin product descriptions or duplicate manufacturer content will struggle if they don't invest in better, more informative content strategies.

AI is also being used in automated SEO tools, making it easier than ever to analyze data, predict ranking shifts, and optimize content. Tools like Surfer SEO and Clearscope use AI to suggest improvements in keyword usage, content structure, and readability. As AI continues to evolve, e-commerce businesses that leverage these tools will have a significant advantage in creating content that aligns with search engine expectations.

Voice Search Optimization for Online Stores

With the rise of smart assistants like Amazon Alexa, Google Assistant, and Apple's Siri, voice search is becoming an increasingly important factor in SEO. More people are using voice commands to find products, compare prices, and even complete purchases, which means e-commerce businesses need to start optimizing for voice search.

Voice searches tend to be longer and more conversational than traditional text-based queries. Instead of searching for "best running shoes," a voice search might be "What are the best running shoes for long-distance runners?" This means optimizing for long-tail keywords and natural language will become essential.

Another major shift is the importance of FAQ-style content. Since voice search queries often take the form of a question, structuring content to answer common customer questions can improve visibility. Creating detailed product FAQs, writing blog posts that answer specific user queries, and incorporating structured data (like FAQ Schema) can help your store rank for voice searches.

Additionally, since many voice searches are local in nature, optimizing for local SEO will be crucial. If you have a physical storefront, make sure your

Google Business Profile is fully optimized and that your store appears in local search results when people search for products near them.

The Rise of Zero-Click Searches & Featured Snippets

One of the biggest challenges facing SEO in recent years is the rise of zero-click searches. These are searches where Google provides an answer directly in the search results, meaning users don't even need to click on a website to get the information they need.

For example, if someone searches "How to clean a leather wallet," they might see a featured snippet at the top of the search results that provides a step-by-step answer without requiring them to click on a website. While this can be frustrating for businesses, there are still ways to benefit from zero-click searches.

The key is to optimize for featured snippets. Google often pulls snippet content from well-structured, authoritative pages that clearly answer a user's question. To improve your chances of getting featured:

- Write content that directly answers common questions.

- Use clear, structured formatting, such as bullet points and numbered lists.

- Incorporate headings (H2 and H3 tags) that match commonly searched phrases.

For e-commerce stores, product comparison tables, how-to guides, and FAQ sections are excellent candidates for featured snippets. If your content is selected as a featured snippet, it can dramatically increase brand visibility and drive traffic, even without a direct click.

How to Stay Ahead in a Constantly Changing SEO Landscape

If there's one thing I've learned in SEO, it's that the only constant is change. Google's algorithms evolve constantly, new ranking factors emerge, and consumer behavior shifts with technological advancements. The best way to future-proof your e-commerce SEO strategy is to stay adaptable and proactive.

First and foremost, focus on user experience. Google has made it clear that sites that provide the best experience – whether through fast loading speeds, mobile-friendly designs, or valuable content – will rank higher. Make sure your site is optimized for both desktop and mobile users, and continuously monitor your site's performance with tools like Google Search Console and Google Analytics.

Keeping up with SEO trends also means staying informed. I always recommend following reputable SEO blogs and industry leaders, such as Moz, Search Engine Journal, and Google's official webmaster blog. These resources provide insights into the latest algorithm updates and best practices.

Additionally, experimenting and testing different SEO strategies is crucial. SEO isn't a one-size-fits-all solution – what works for one business might not work for another. Running A/B tests on product pages, testing different title tags, and analyzing heatmaps can help identify what resonates best with your audience.

Lastly, don't ignore new search technologies. As AI, voice search, and structured data continue to shape the search landscape, businesses that embrace these changes will have a competitive advantage. Investing in video content, optimizing for voice search, and leveraging AI-driven SEO tools can help keep your store at the forefront of search visibility.

**

The future of SEO in e-commerce is full of opportunities, but only for those who are willing to adapt, innovate, and evolve. AI and machine learning are reshaping search algorithms, voice search is changing the way customers find products, and zero-click searches are altering how traffic flows from search engines to websites.

The key takeaway is this: focus on providing value to your customers. Whether through high-quality content, seamless user experiences, or forward-thinking SEO strategies, businesses that prioritize their audience's needs will continue to succeed – no matter how search engines change.

As we wrap up this book, I encourage you to

take action. SEO isn't about waiting for results – it's about continuous optimization, learning from data, and staying ahead of the curve. The businesses that thrive in the future will be the ones that embrace change, test new strategies, and always keep their customers at the center of everything they do.

CONCLUSION & NEXT STEPS

When I first started working with e-commerce SEO, I quickly realized that success wasn't about mastering a single tactic – it was about consistently applying a strategic approach over time. SEO isn't just about rankings; it's about building a sustainable source of organic traffic that drives sales and grows your business long-term. If there's one thing I want you to take away from this book, it's that SEO is an investment, not a quick fix. The more effort you put in now, the more your store will benefit down the road.

Recap of Key Strategies

Throughout this book, we've covered a wide range of SEO strategies, from the fundamentals of keyword research to advanced link-building and technical optimizations. The core takeaway is that SEO success requires a multi-layered approach. Let's quickly revisit the most important strategies:

Keyword Optimization: Understanding the intent behind search queries and structuring your content around buyer-focused keywords is crucial. Avoid keyword cannibalization and focus on long-tail phrases that attract high-intent shoppers.

On-Page SEO: Every product and category page should be fully optimized with compelling titles, engaging descriptions, and high-quality images that help both search engines and users.

Technical SEO: Site speed, mobile-friendliness, structured data, and proper site architecture play a huge role in rankings and user experience.

Content Marketing: Blogging, buying guides, and video content are powerful ways to attract organic traffic while also positioning your brand as an industry leader.

Link Building: Earning backlinks from reputable sources – whether through guest posts, digital PR, influencer collaborations, or supplier partnerships – helps establish credibility and boosts domain authority.

SEO Analytics & Performance Monitoring: Tracking metrics like rankings, traffic, CTR, bounce rate, and conversions allows you to continually refine your approach.

Future-Proofing Your SEO: Adapting to AI-driven algorithms, voice search, zero-click searches, and structured data ensures your store remains competitive as SEO evolves.

If you've followed along and implemented these strategies, you've already built a solid SEO foundation for your online store. Now, it's about continuing to refine and scale your efforts over time.

Recommended Tools & Resources

One of the best things about SEO is that there are incredible tools available to help streamline and improve your efforts. Here are some of the essential tools I recommend for ongoing SEO success:

Google Search Console – Track keyword rankings, search performance, and indexing issues.

Google Analytics 4 – Monitor organic traffic, user behavior, and conversion data.

Ahrefs / SEMrush / Moz – Conduct in-depth keyword research, track backlinks, and analyze competitors.

Screaming Frog – Identify technical SEO issues like broken links, duplicate content, and site speed problems.

Surfer SEO / Clearscope – Optimize content with AI-driven recommendations for keywords and readability.

Hotjar / Lucky Orange – Use heatmaps and session recordings to analyze how users interact with your site.

TinyPNG / ShortPixel – Optimize images to improve site speed.

These tools will help you continuously track, analyze, and optimize your SEO strategy, ensuring that your store remains visible and competitive in search results.

Developing an SEO-First

Mindset in E-Commerce

One of the biggest challenges I see with e-commerce store owners is treating SEO as an afterthought. Many businesses invest heavily in paid advertising and social media but neglect the long-term power of organic traffic.

Adopting an SEO-first mindset means making search engine optimization a core part of every business decision. When launching a new product, consider how customers will search for it. When designing your website, think about how Google will crawl and index it. When creating content, ensure it aligns with real user search intent.

SEO is never truly "done." It's a process of constant improvement, testing, and adaptation. Google's algorithms evolve, competitors adjust their strategies, and consumer behavior shifts. The businesses that succeed in organic search are those that stay proactive – always optimizing, always learning, and always improving.

SEO is one of the most valuable assets your e-commerce business can have. Unlike paid ads, where traffic disappears the moment you stop spending, a well-optimized site will continue attracting customers month after month, year after year.

Moving Forward

Now that you've built a strong understanding of e-commerce SEO, it's time to put it into action.

Start by prioritizing the strategies that will have the biggest impact on your store. If your product pages need work, optimize them first. If you haven't invested in content marketing, start planning a blog strategy. If you're unsure how well your site is performing, conduct a full SEO audit and track key metrics.

Success in SEO doesn't happen overnight, but with persistence and consistency, you'll see results. Keep testing, keep learning, and keep optimizing. The effort you put in today will pay off in the form of increased visibility, more organic traffic, and higher sales for years to come.

ABOUT THE AUTHOR

Danielle Mead

Danielle Mead is an e-commerce expert with over 25 years of experience working at dotcom startups and as an independent web designer and consultant. She has worked with over 600 clients across industries to launch and optimize online stores that deliver results. Her one-woman company, Duck Soup E-Commerce, primarily works with clients on the BigCommerce platform, empowering online retailers with practical tools and strategies to overcome challenges and succeed in competitive markets. She is passionate about simplifying the complexities of e-commerce and creating clear, actionable plans for success. Learn more about Danielle and her services at her website https://ducksoupecommerce.com.

SEO For E-Commerce Unlocked is your ultimate guide to optimizing your website, increasing organic traffic, and converting visitors into loyal customers. Whether you're a small business owner, a digital marketer, or a store developer, you'll learn practical, actionable SEO techniques tailored specifically for online stores.

Danielle Mead is an e-commerce expert with over 25 years of experience working at dotcom startups and as an independent web designer and consultant. She has worked with over 600 clients across industries through her one-woman company, Duck Soup E-Commerce, which specializes in the BigCommerce platform. She is passionate about simplifying the complexities of e-commerce and creating clear, actionable plans for success.

ISBN 9798314710753

9 798314 710753

90000